S.T.E.A.M. AHEAD

Experiment
— with —
OUTDOOR
SCIENCE

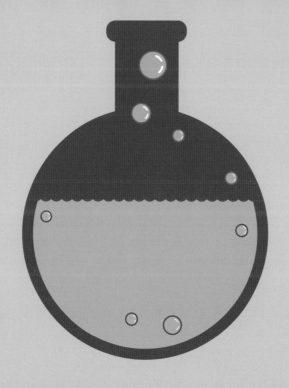

Quarto is the authority on a wide range of topics.

Quarto educates, entertains and enriches the lives of our readers—enthusiasts and lovers of hands-on living.

www.quartoknows.com

Author: Nick Arnold
Illustrator: Giulia Zoavo
Design and Editorial: Starry Dog Books Ltd
Consultant: Pete Robinson

© 2021 Quarto Publishing plc

First Published in 2020 by QEB Publishing,
an imprint of The Quarto Group.
26391 Crown Valley Parkway,
Suite 220
Mission Viejo, CA 92691, USA
T: +1 949 380 7510
F: +1 949 380 7575
www.QuartoKnows.com

A CIP record for this book is available from the Library of Congress.

ISBN 978-0-7112-4398-9

Manufactured in Guangdong, China TT052021

9 8 7 6 5 4 3 2 1

Picture credits
All photographs by Starry Dog Books Ltd
with the exception of the following:

Alamy 27 tilt&shift / Stockimo / Alamy Stock Photo

Fiona Hayes 42-43

Shutterstock 8-9 b/g thidaphon taoha; 10-11 b/g ifong; 12-13 Sergey Nivens, 12-13 b/g sumroeng chinnapan; 16-17 b/g sumroeng chinnapan; 18-19 b/g Evgeny Atamanenko; 20-21 b/g keeplight; 22-23 b/g Pipochka; 28-29 b/g keeplight; 39 epsilon_lyrae, 39 b/g Pooh photo; 41b (clockwise from top) a) domnitsky, b) Tamara Kulikova, c) Nipaporn Panyacharoen; 44-45 New Africa, 45tl oksana2010, 45tc oksana2010; 48-49 Sergei Mironenko; 52br pzAxe, 52-53 b/g dugdax, 53 (woodlouse) ch123; 56/57 b/g keeplight; 59 Andreas Hvidsten; 66-67 b/g cooperr; 68-69 b/g Vivo e verde; 72-73 b/g dIsk, 73b jannoon028; 77 (hand) Bloomicon, 77 b/g Erkki Makkonen.

Superstock 37 Radius

S.T.E.A.M. AHEAD

Experiment
— with —
OUTDOOR
SCIENCE

Nick Arnold

QEB

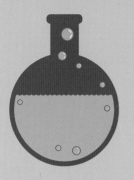

CONTENTS

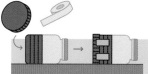

CHAPTER 4: BUGS AND BIRDS

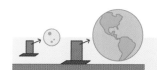

CHAPTER 5: SKY AND SPACE

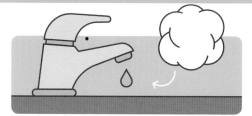

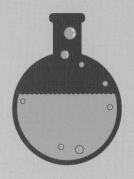

INTRODUCTION

The world's biggest science lab is right outside your window. Yes, the great outdoors is full of moving things, living things, and wild weather. There's plenty of room for BIG experiments, maximum mess, and shout-out-loud FUN! Let's get started...

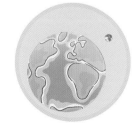

Golden rules
FOR SENSIBLE SCIENTISTS

Rule 1
BE ORGANIZED
Before you start an experiment, read the instructions and make sure you have everything you need handy.

Look out for the circles—they contain handy hints that help to make the experiments work better.

Rule 2
BE SAFE!
Ask for adult help whenever you see this symbol. Always follow the WARNING! advice in the red boxes. Don't go anywhere alone, especially at night. Don't eat wild plants; they may be toxic. Don't handle creatures such as bugs or spiders unless an adult has told you they're safe.

ASK AN ADULT

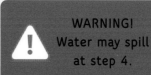

WARNING! Water may spill at step 4.

Rule 3
BE TIDY!
Tidy up after each experiment and throw away or recycle waste materials. Look for the yellow MESS WARNING! boxes and follow the advice.

MESS WARNING! Waterproof pens can mark hands and clothes.

THINK GREEN AND RECYCLE!

Many of the projects in this book provide a great way to recycle plastic items; wherever possible, try to find the items you need at home rather than buying new products. When you have finished, recycle any plastic items. That way you can help to keep plastic out of landfills.

You can try these experiments in any order, but the science explanations make more sense if you tackle them in the order they appear in this book.

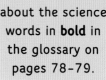

You can find out about the science words in **bold** in the glossary on pages 78-79.

CHAPTER 1: MOVING MOMENTS

FLOAT YOUR BOATS

Enjoy a boat trip in your own backyard with a bobbing bottle boat and, on the next page, a folded paper boat that floats!

WARNING!
DON'T float your boats in ponds, rivers, lakes, or canals.

3 Roll a 1-inch (2.5-cm) wide ball of modeling clay and press it into the boat, making sure it's in the center. Stick a drinking straw into the modeling clay and secure it with thin tape.

1 Ask an adult to make a cut (A) in the side of a 16.9-ounce (500 ml) plastic bottle. Cut out the rest of the rectangle.

ASK AN ADULT

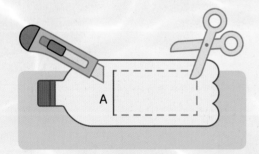

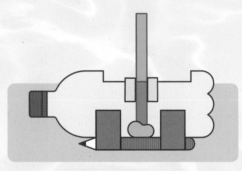

2 Use packing tape to attach a pen to the opposite side of the bottle.

The pen must be straight and exactly in the center of the uncut side.

4 To make the sail, cut the end off a short envelope. Use a sharp pencil to make a hole in the uncut end, then slide the envelope onto the straw.

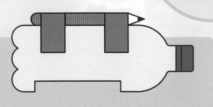

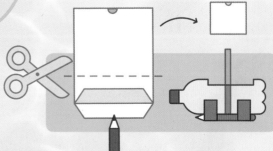

You will need...

- 16.9 ounce (500 ml) plastic screw-top bottle
- Knife
- Scissors
- Pen
- Packing tape
- Modeling clay
- Drinking straw
- Tape
- Short envelope
- Sharp pencil

5 Your boat is ready to launch. If it leans to one side on the water, simply straighten the mast until the boat is upright. Blow gently on the sail to move the boat along.

Float your boat in a wading pool or large container of water.

The Science: FLOATING

A force called gravity pushes the boat down into the water, but the water pushes back just as hard: this is a force called upthrust. Your boat floats, or is **buoyant**, because the water it pushes aside weighs the same as the boat.

You can make a paper boat by folding just one sheet of paper! Then have fun decorating it.

You will need...

- Printer size paper (ideally waxed paper)
- Pen
- Ruler
- Scissors
- Colored pens
- Tape
- Thick cardstock
- Adhesive putty

1 Fold the paper in half, top to bottom. Then fold it left to right and unfold again to leave a central crease.

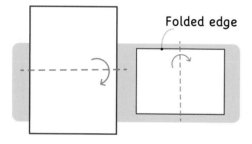

Folded edge

2 Turn down the top corners so they meet at the central crease. Turn up the bottom sections, one to the front and one to the back. Tuck the ends over so you have a triangle shape.

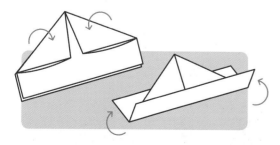

3 Push ends A and B toward each other, making a diamond shape.

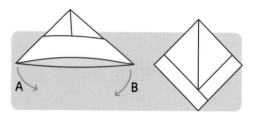

A   B

4 Fold the bottom corner up to meet the top corner. Repeat on the other side, making a triangle shape.

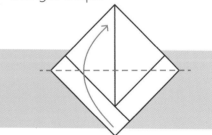

5 Push corners C and D down to meet each other, making another diamond. Pull tips E and F apart, and a boat will magically appear!

E   F

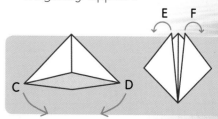

C   D

6 To make the keel, which gives a boat stability, cut this shape from thick cardstock. Cover it with tape to make it waterproof. Push the wide end up into the fold on the bottom of the boat and attach it with tape.

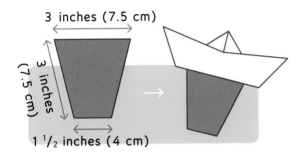

3 inches (7.5 cm)

3 inches (7.5 cm)

1 ¹/₂ inches (4 cm)

7 Decorate your boat. If you did not use waxed paper, waterproof the sides by covering them with tape. Launch your boat!

The Science: DRAG AND STREAMLINING

Compare how your boats sail. As a boat moves through water, a rubbing force called **friction** slows it down. This is the same force that heats your hands when you rub them. In water or air, this force is called **drag**. The paper boat is more streamlined than the bottle boat—its pointed front allows water to pass more easily along its sides, and this reduces drag.

Your boat floats best with small weights aboard. If it leans to one side, try to balance it by placing a blob of adhesive putty on the other side.

MASSIVE MEGAPHONES

Listen up! The only thing better than shouting outdoors is SHOUTING EVEN LOUDER outdoors. Here's how to do it...

1 Take a large sheet of paper, and measure and mark the mid-point on the two short sides.

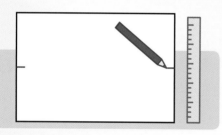

2 Use a compass to draw a curved line next to each of the two points, as shown.

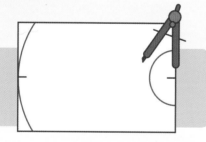

At step 2 you could use a pencil and piece of string to draw the curved lines.

3 Use a ruler to draw lines A and B from the ends of line C to the opposite mid-point. Cut along lines A and B, then cut along lines C and D.

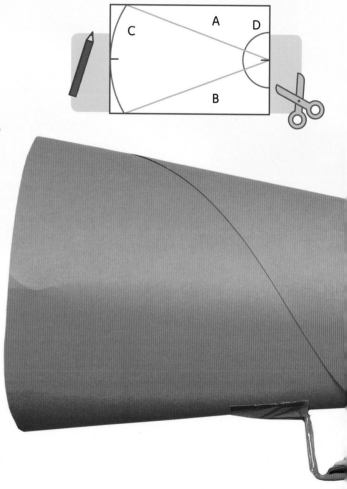

You will need...

- 2 large sheets of construction paper or thin cardstock
- Ruler
- Pencil
- Compass
- Scissors
- Wide tape
- Strip of cardstock

The Science: SOUND WAVES

The energy of your shout causes vibrations in the air called **sound waves**. We detect sound waves using our ears and our brains. Normally sound waves spread out in all directions, but a megaphone channels them in one direction. Your friend hears a louder sound because your megaphone channels the sound waves toward them, and their own megaphone channels the sound waves directly into their ear.

4 Cut 4 or 5 pieces of tape. Roll the paper lengthways to make a cone-shaped tube; overlap the sides and secure them with tape. The gap at the narrow end should measure 1–2 inches (2.5–5 cm) across.

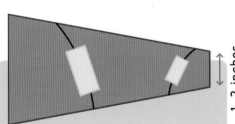

1–2 inches (2.5–5 cm)

5 To make a handle, take a long strip of cardstock and score and bend it to make this shape. Tape the handle halfway along the megaphone.

6 Repeat steps 1–5 to make a second megaphone.

7 Ask a friend to hold one of the megaphones 13 feet (4 m) away from you. They should put the narrow end to their ear and point the wide end at you. Now shout into your own megaphone. Test your two megaphones at ever-increasing distances.

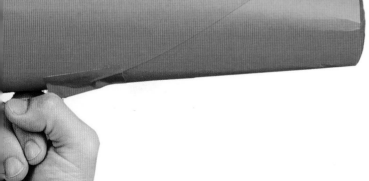

MAKE A PARACHUTE

Do heights make your legs go wobbly?
Now you can make and test a parachute
WITHOUT plunging from a plane!

WARNING!
DON'T climb anywhere high
unless you are with an adult.
DON'T drop your parachute
from a window that has
people or traffic beneath it.

1 Fold a plastic
garbage bag into
quarters. Draw
a curve above
the corner where
both folds join,
as shown.

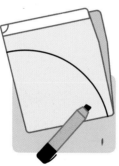

2 Ask an adult to cut along the curve
through all four layers of plastic.
This will give you two large plastic
circles. Discard one of them.

ASK AN
ADULT

DID YOU KNOW?

Air resistance stops a human
from falling faster than about
125 miles (200 km) per hour.
This is called terminal velocity.

3 Take your plastic circle and fold
eight sticky labels over the outer
edge, an equal distance apart.
Punch a hole through each label.

4 Measure and cut eight 6-foot
(180 cm) lengths of string.

5 Fold one of the lengths of string in
half. Push the looped end through
one of the holes from underneath,
thread the two ends through the
loop, then pull them tight. Repeat
for the other seven holes.

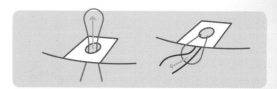

You will need...

- Plastic garbage bag
- Marker
- Scissors
- Sticky labels
- Hole puncher
- Tape measure
- String
- Curtain ring, paperclip, or small toy

6 Gather the strings together so their ends are level and tie them in one big knot to the curtain ring, or you could try using a small toy. Your parachute is ready to test out!

If you don't have a hole puncher, you can make the holes using a sharp pencil.

The Science:
GRAVITY AND DRAG

The force of gravity pulls any object with **mass** toward the Earth. As the parachute falls, its large surface area traps trillions of air **molecules**, which push back and produce drag. This is called air resistance.

It makes the parachute fall at a slow and steady terminal velocity.

Air resistance

Gravity

KITE FLIGHT

Take creative science to new heights with this simple kite design. Then watch your kite catch the breeze and soar up into the sky!

1 Take a large plastic sheet and draw on this kite shape, starting with the rectangle. Cut the shape out.

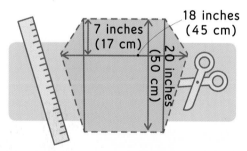

7 inches (17 cm)

18 inches (45 cm)

20 inches (50 cm)

2 Use small scissors to cut out two 3 ½-inch (9-cm) wide circles. The center of each circle should be 5 inches (12 cm) from the bottom edge.

5 inches (12 cm)

It may help to draw around a circular object.

3 To make the struts, stick two pencils together end to end using duct tape. Repeat for the other two pairs of pencils. Tape the struts to the kite, as shown. Wrap a piece of duct tape around corners A and B.

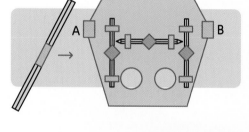

A

B

4 Ask an adult to make a hole through the duct tape on corners A and B using a sharp pencil. Cut a 33-inch (85-cm) length of string and tie the ends securely to the holes.

ASK AN ADULT

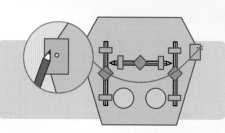

You will need...

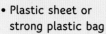

- Plastic sheet or strong plastic bag
- Pen
- Ruler
- Large scissors
- Small scissors
- Duct tape
- 6 pencils for struts
- Metal ring or paperclip
- Sharp pencil
- Strong string or twine

The Science: LIFT

The wind pushes on the kite, but the string stops it from moving away. Instead the string makes the kite tilt at an angle to the wind and pushes the air downward. This produces an upward force called **lift**, which raises the kite in the air. By pulling the kite toward you, you can increase this force and raise the kite higher.

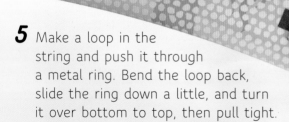

Instead of pairs of pencils, you could use wooden dowels for the struts.

5 Make a loop in the string and push it through a metal ring. Bend the loop back, slide the ring down a little, and turn it over bottom to top, then pull tight.

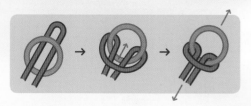

6 Cut a 66-foot (20-m) length of string and tie one end to the metal ring. Take your kite outside on a windy day. Stand with your back to the wind, hold the kite high, and let it go, but keep hold of the string! With luck your kite will fly high!

FLYING DISK

Put science in a spin with your very own flying disk...

1 Roll five $\frac{1}{2}$-inch (1.2-cm) wide blobs of adhesive putty. Stick four of them onto the rim of a plastic plate an equal distance apart. Put the fifth blob in the center.

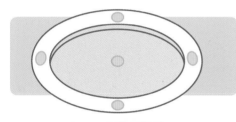

3 Tape the rims tightly together.

2 Press the second plate onto the first one, taking care not to break the rims.

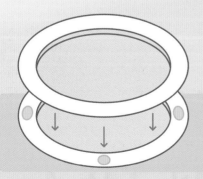

You will need...

- Two light plastic plates (at least 8 inches/20 cm diameter)
- Adhesive putty
- Tape
- Pens to decorate

The Science:
BERNOULLI PRINCIPLE AND ANGULAR MOMENTUM

Your flying disk flies well for two reasons. First, its shape produces lift, which keeps it in the air. Here's what happens:

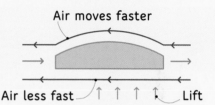

Air moves faster

Air less fast ↑ ↑ ↑ ↑ Lift

4 Try out your flying disk on a windless day. Stand side-on to the direction you want to throw the disk, hold it level, quickly move it forward, and release it with a backwards flick of the wrist.

You could decorate your flying disk using colored pens.

The Bernoulli Principle states that when a gas or fluid speeds up, its pressure drops. Since air moves faster over the disk's upper surface, the **air pressure** is higher on the lower surface. The difference in air pressure produces lift.

The second reason your flying disk flies so well is because spin keeps it stable in the air. The steady spin is due to a quality called **angular momentum**. The more mass and the faster the disk spins, the greater its angular momentum. The adhesive putty inside your flying disk increases its mass and boosts its angular momentum, making it fly better.

Flying disk challenge

Which throw makes the flying disk go farthest?
a) Disk held level with spin
b) Disk tilted downward
c) Disk tilted upward
d) Disk held level but no spin

Answer:
a) Can you explain your results in terms of lift and angular momentum (see The Science)?

GETTING IN A SPIN

How can you turn a sheet of paper into a helicopter that spins? Let's find out! The bigger you make it, the better it will work.

1 Cut out a rectangle of cardstock; make the width one-third of the length. Draw on the cutting lines (blue) and fold lines (red). Cut along the cutting lines.

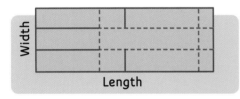

Width

Length

2 To make the tail—the part that sticks down—fold A and B in, then fold the bottom section over.

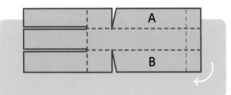

A

B

3 Fold C and D in so they form a triangular section. Secure with tape.

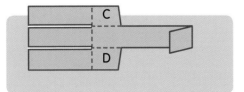

C

D

4 Fold the three rotors down as shown.

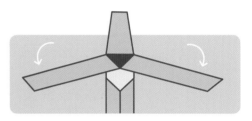

5 Now hold your helicopter as high as you can, throw it up into the air, and watch it come spinning back down.

Make sure all the folds are sharp. If your spinner doesn't spin, try unfolding the flap at the bottom and folding it up again. It may help to twist the rotors so their ends point slightly downward; twist each one in the same direction.

Scoring along the dotted lines will make the cardstock easier to fold.

The Science:
DRAG, SPIN, AND AIRFOILS

Helicopter engines spin their rotors very fast. The rotors have an **airfoil** shape and a slight twist that together produce maximum lift.

Air moves faster over upper surface

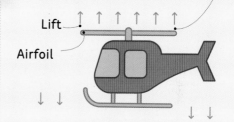

Lift

Airfoil

Air sweeps downward producing more lift

Helicopter challenge

What do you think will happen if you attach a paperclip to the tail?

a) It will spin faster
b) It will spin slower
c) It won't spin at all

Answer: a)

Your paper helicopter doesn't generate lift. Instead, gravity pulls it down in a straight line. As it falls, the upward force of air on the twisted rotors causes the helicopter to spin. The rotors produce drag, slowing the helicopter's fall.

SNOWBALL FLIGHT TESTS

Try out these wet and dry snowballs to see which flies farthest. Who says scientists don't have fun?

1 Bundle together a handful of cotton balls to make a snowball. Now make a second snowball the same size as the first one—use a ruler to check they are the same size.

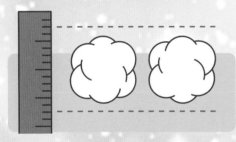

2 Put one ball under a faucet until it is damp but not soaking wet.

3 Wrap both balls in plastic wrap.

4 Throw each ball in the same direction with the same force. Which goes farthest?

You may like to throw the balls at a friend and invite them to throw them back!

If it's snowy, try this experiment with real snow! The best snow for snowballs is slightly damp, so look for snow that has the sun on it or is near a building. It will refreeze when you make it into a snowball. To give one ball more mass, pack more snow into it, but take care to make both your snowballs the same size.

The Science:
DRAG, MASS, AND MOMENTUM

As the balls fly through the air, the air resistance (drag) slows them down. Eventually gravity pulls the snowballs back down to Earth. The damp ball has more mass than the dry ball, which means the damp ball has more **momentum**. Drag takes longer to slow it down, so it travels farther.

This is a comparison experiment. Two objects—in this case balls—are exactly the same apart from one change, so any difference in what happens to the objects must be due to this change. In a comparison experiment, the object that isn't changed is called the control.

WHAT GOES AROUND COMES APART

Before we get mixing, let's try separating substances. It's as easy as spinning a wheel!

1 Quarter-fill a $\frac{1}{2}$-ounce (15-ml) bottle with olive oil. Fill the rest of the bottle with white vinegar.

2 Pour the mixture into a bowl. Add one-third of a teaspoon of smooth mustard. Stir until the mustard has disappeared. Put the mixture back into the bottle and screw on the lid.

3 Photograph the bottle from the side and from below. Can you see any mustard?

4 **ASK AN ADULT** Ask an adult to help you tape the bottle firmly to two of the spokes on the back wheel of a bicycle.

5 **ASK AN ADULT** Ask an adult to put on goggles and gloves. They should set the bike to a high gear, turn it upside down, and turn one of the pedals as fast as they can for one minute, then stop the wheel using the brakes.

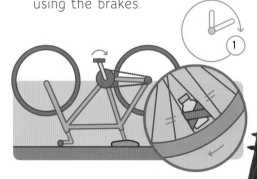

You will need...

- Clean ½-ounce (15-ml) screw-top plastic bottle
- Olive oil
- White vinegar
- Bowl
- Smooth mustard
- Teaspoon
- Camera
- Bicycle
- Duct tape or strong packing tape
- Scissors
- Goggles
- Thick gloves

DID YOU KNOW?

A centrifuge machine separates mixtures by spinning. Medical scientists use them to separate the ingredients of blood.

The Science: CENTRIPETAL, CENTRIFUGAL

Olive oil is lighter than vinegar, so it floats, but mustard stops olive oil from forming a floating layer. When you add mustard, the mixture stays mixed up.

As you spin the mixture, it tries to fly off in a straight line. This is called **centrifugal effect**. But the wheel rim provides a **centripetal force** that pushes the mixture toward the center of the wheel. Centrifugal effect depends on an object's mass: the greater the mass, the bigger the effect. Since the molecules in mustard and vinegar are more massive than in olive oil, they are pushed harder toward the wheel and the mixture separates.

6 Cut the duct tape and remove the bottle. Now compare the mixture with your photographs from step 3. Can you see olive oil at the top of the mixture and mustard at the bottom?

MAKE GIANT BUBBLES

When bubbles get super-sized, so does the fun! Here's how to make big bubbles, and EVEN BIGGER bubbles!

1 Put 7 ounces (200 ml) of hot tap water into a 16.9-ounce (500-ml) screw-top bottle. Add 1 $\frac{1}{2}$ tablespoons of glycerine and enough dishwashing liquid to fill the bottle to the brim.

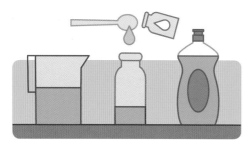

2 Screw the lid on tight and shake the bottle for 20 seconds. Then leave it for at least 3 days. Cool the mixture in the fridge for at least one hour.

3 Cut a plastic drinking straw in half. Thread a 24-inch (60-cm) length of string through both pieces of straw and knot the string. This is your smaller bubble wand.

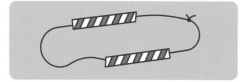

4 For even bigger bubbles, cut two pieces of string, 39 inches (1 m) and 47 inches (1.2 m) long. Tie the ends of the shorter string to the ends of two long sticks. Tie the longer string to the first string, as shown.

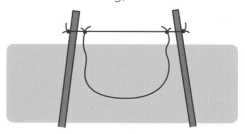

5 Pour the bubble mixture into a large bowl. Take your smaller wand and, holding the straws together, dip it into the mixture until the string is soaked. Open the straws and sweep the bubble wand around to release a bubble. Now try this with the larger wands!

DID YOU KNOW?

In 2006 Sam Heath blew a giant bubble around 19 boys and girls!

You will need...

- Measuring jug
- Water
- 16.9-ounce (500-ml) screw-top bottle
- Tablespoon
- Glycerine
- Dishwashing liquid
- Plastic drinking straw
- Scissors
- Thin string
- Tape measure
- Two long sticks
- Large bowl

The Science:
BUBBLE WALLS AND EVAPORATION

As you separate the wands, a thin film of detergent and water forms between the strings. The air makes this film bulge. As you move the wands, the film snaps around the air to make a bubble; it squeezes the bubble into the smallest area it can, which is always a sphere. The bubble wall is like a water and detergent sandwich.

Detergent ———————— Water

When some of the water molecules **evaporate**, the wall weakens and pops. Glycerine thickens the detergent layers, so the water can't evaporate as easily. Becasue the bubbles have stronger walls, you can blow bigger, longer-lasting bubbles. Cool bubbles don't burst as easily either. This is because water evaporates less quickly in cooler air.

This experiment works best on a windless day.

BLOW A BUBBLE SNAKE

Have fun making a giant bubble snake—one that can fly! The secret is knowing how to make bubbles stick together!

WARNING!
Be careful not to breathe in the bubble mixture.

2 Pull a sock over the cut end so part of the sock is tight against the cut end. Secure the sock with duct tape.

1 Take the top off a bottle. Ask an adult to cut off the bottom fifth of the bottle.

ASK AN ADULT

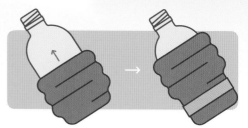

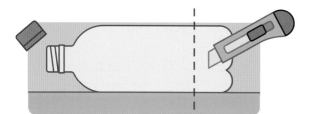

DID YOU KNOW?

Whipped cream is a form of foam. The bubbles last a long time because the bubble walls contain milk fat.

You will need...

- 16.9-ounce (500-ml) plastic bottle
- Knife or scissors
- Duct tape or large rubber band
- Old sock
- Bubble mixture (see page 26, steps 1–2)
- Food coloring (optional)

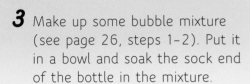

3 Make up some bubble mixture (see page 26, steps 1–2). Put it in a bowl and soak the sock end of the bottle in the mixture.

4 Hold the bottle near the ground and blow into it with short, hard puffs. Out of the sock a long bubble snake will emerge!

To make a colorful snake, dip the sock in food coloring before you blow into the bottle!

The Science: AIR PRESSURE AND SURFACE TENSION

The bubbles that make up your snake are filled with air from your lungs. They're small because they emerge through small holes in the sock. There's also some water on the outside of the bubbles. Water molecules are drawn together by a force called **surface tension**. This helps the bubbles to stick together, making foam. The long-lasting bubble mixture ensures that the bubble snake holds together.

Bubble snake challenge

1) Can you blow a bubble snake longer than 3 feet (91 cm)?
2) Make a flying bubble snake! Hold the blower up high when you puff into it (it works best when there's a slight breeze).
3) How high can your snake fly?

VOLCANIC ERUPTIONS

Imagine a volcano erupting in your garden! This one oozes masses of red lava. Then turn the page for an explosive eruption!

 MESS WARNING!
Food coloring stains! Wear old clothes and set up the experiment on bare earth.

1 Put a small pot, open end down, in the bottom of a bucket. Press sand into the bucket. If the sand is dry, sprinkle on a little water.

2 Turn out a sandcastle.

3 Measure out 13.5 ounces (400 ml) of vinegar. Add enough red food coloring to make a strong red color.

4 Measure out ½ cup (130 g) of baking soda. Press sand onto the inside of the pot at the top of your sandcastle to hide it. Pour the baking soda into the pot.

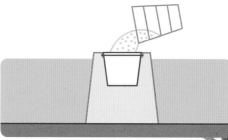

ICE VOLCANO

If you don't have sand, use ice! Put a small pot, open end down, in a bucket. Put a plastic bag in the bucket, tucking it around the pot, and fill with water. Freeze for 24 hours. Take the bag out of the bucket and peel it off the ice. Follow steps 3 to 5, putting the baking soda into the hollow in the ice left by the pot.

Always wear gloves when handling ice.

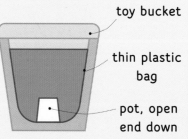

toy bucket

thin plastic bag

pot, open end down

You will need...

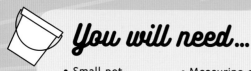

- Small pot
- Kid's beach bucket
- Sand
- Water
- 13.5 ounces (400 ml) white vinegar or lemon juice
- Measuring cup
- Red food coloring
- $\frac{1}{2}$ cup (130 g) baking soda
- Kitchen scales

5 Trickle the colored vinegar onto the baking soda and watch as red lava erupts and oozes down the volcano!

The Science:
CHEMICAL REACTIONS: ACIDS AND BASES

You made your volcano erupt by mixing vinegar with baking soda. Vinegar contains an acid; it's at least 4% acetic acid. Baking soda is a base. When mixed with water, both of these chemicals can dissolve other substances, but they aren't strong enough to harm humans! You do notice the acid if you put vinegar on your tongue. The acid makes vinegar taste sour.

When you combined the acid and the base, you created new molecules in what scientists call a **chemical reaction**. The acid and base combined to make water, a salt called sodium ethanoate, and carbon dioxide gas. It's the gas bubbles that make the lava fizz and expand until it flows down the volcano.

You will need...

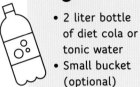

- 2 liter bottle of diet cola or tonic water
- Small bucket (optional)
- Packet of mints (the type with a hole in the middle!)

3 Stand the bottle outside, away from buildings—you can put it in a bucket for stability. Open the bottle very slowly. Try not to let too much gas escape.

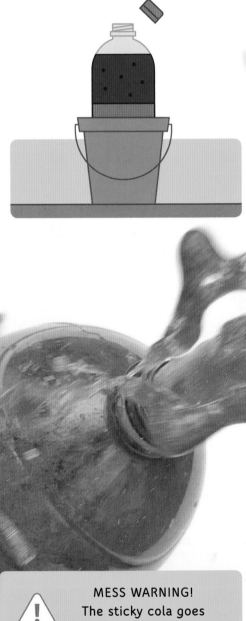

This explosive volcano shoots cola lava high into the air. It's fast and furious, and only lasts a few seconds!

1 Place the cola in a warm place for at least two hours.

2 Unwrap the mints and get four of them ready.

 MESS WARNING! The sticky cola goes everywhere! Wash it away with water.

If you use less than 2 liters of cola, drop in only two mints.

4 As soon as you've taken off the cap, drop four mints into the bottle and quickly step back. The cola lava will shoot high up into the air!

The Science:
BUBBLES, SURFACES, AND REAL VOLCANOES

Unlike the previous experiment, this eruption isn't a chemical reaction; it's a physical change.

The cola drink contains dissolved carbon dioxide gas. The gas is under pressure in the liquid and can't escape. Warming the bottle boosts this pressure. When you add mints, you provide rough surfaces for gas molecules to stick to. The molecules form bubbles. Now they can escape! They rise to the surface very fast, and the escaping gas shoots liquid from the bottle.

Some real volcanoes produce gentle streams of lava. But if there's a lot of gas in the lava, the eruptions can be explosive, just like this one!

SOIL SECRETS

Soil makes a wonderful, muddy mess, but what is it made of and how does it compare to sand? Let's take a close look!

 WARNING!
Soil contains bacteria. Put a bandage on any cuts and wear gloves!

1 Weigh out 3 ½ ounces (100 g) of soil and put it in a saucer.

2 Put 3 ½ ounces (100 g) of sand in a separate saucer.

3 Use a magnifying glass to examine the soil and the sand. What do you see? How are the soil and sand different?

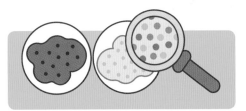

4 Put a coffee filter in a funnel and put the funnel on a jar.

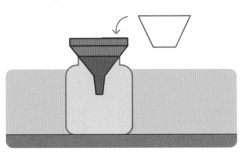

5 Put the soil into the filter paper. Little by little, pour 3 ½ ounces (100 ml) of water over the soil, allowing it to soak through before adding more. Wait five minutes, then measure the height of the water in the jar.

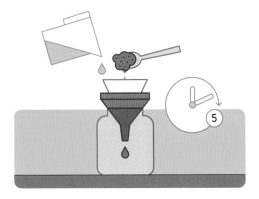

6 Empty the jar and repeat steps 4–5 using sand. Which let the most water through: soil or sand?

You will need...

- Gloves
- 2 small saucers
- Old tablespoon
- Kitchen scales
- Soil
- Sand
- Magnifying glass

- 2 coffee filter papers
- Large funnel
- Glass jar
- Water
- Measuring cup
- Ruler

The Science:
SOIL STRUCTURE AND MOISTURE RETENTION

Like the snowball activity on pages 22–23, this is a comparison experiment. The aim was to discover which sample retained most moisture.

At step 3, you saw that sand is made of grains (tiny stones), while soil consists of crumbs made of smaller grains stuck together. When you poured water over the sand, the water slipped between the stones and nearly all of it ended up in the jar. But when you poured water on the soil, the water soaked into the crumbs and coated the tiny soil grains. Far less water reached the jar. Soil is like a sponge: it soaks up water and stays moist, even in dry weather.

Soil challenge

1) Why do plants grow better in soil than in sand?
2) What would happen to plants and animals if there were no soil?

Answers:
1) Soil retains water, and plants need water to survive.
2) Plants would die, and without plants to eat most animals would starve.

GROW POTATOES

Did you know you can grow a potato plant from a potato? Here's how to do it!

WARNING!
Soil contains bacteria. Put a bandage on any cuts on your hands, and wear gloves!

1 Wash and dry a potato and leave it in a dark place for a few days until its "eyes" start to sprout. Ask an adult to cut the potato in half as shown.

ASK AN ADULT

2 Push 4 toothpicks into one half of the potato, halfway up the sides.

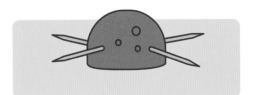

3 Fill a jar with water. Rest the toothpicks on the rim so that the cut side of the potato is underwater. Put the jar in a light place.

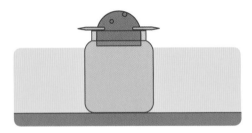

4 Keep the water topped up. After a few days, roots and shoots will appear.

5 Put 1-2 inches (2.5-5 cm) of small stones into a clean plant pot. Add potting compost to fill one third of the pot. Put the potato on it, cut side down. Cover it with about 3 inches (7.5 cm) of potting compost.

You will need...

- Gloves
- Potato
- Knife
- Toothpicks
- Glass jar
- Water
- Plant pot
- Small stones
- Potting compost or garden soil

The best potatoes to use are seed potatoes from a garden center or organic potatoes.

6 Water the compost until it is moist but not soggy. In a few days, the shoots will push up through the compost. Keep adding more compost until the pot is full. After several months, your potato plant should produce potatoes!

Choose a potato with lots of "eyes" —these are buds that will sprout new shoots.

The Science: VEGETATIVE REPRODUCTION

Everyone knows that new plants grow from seeds. But new plants can also grow from bits of old plants, without seeds or flowers. This is called vegetative reproduction. The new plants are copies of the original plant. Some simple animals can grow new parts too, but complex animals, such as humans, cannot. If they could, scientists could grow new humans from body bits!

A potato is a tuber—a living structure produced in the roots. It is rich in a substance called starch. The shoots of the potato plant grow using food energy in the starch.

GROWING CUTTINGS

Here's how to turn one pretty plant into lots of plants! This experiment is best done in spring or summer, when plants are growing.

1 Ask an adult to cut the top 3–4 inches (7.5–10 cm) from a growing shoot, just below a leaf. The shoot should be young and green, not old and woody.

ASK AN ADULT

2 Remove any leaves from the bottom 1 inch (2.5 cm) of the cutting, and put it in a jar with 1 inch (2.5 cm) of water. Keep the water topped up, and after 3 to 4 weeks, roots will appear. When the roots are 2 inches (5 cm) long, the cutting is ready to plant.

3 Put some small stones in a flowerpot. Wearing gloves, fill the pot with compost to about ¹/₂ inch (1.2 cm) below the rim.

4 Make a hole in the compost with a pencil and stand the cutting in the hole. Gently pack compost around the roots.

5 Stand the pot on a saucer. Add water to the pot, up to the brim.

6 Cover the pot and cutting with a plastic bag secured with a rubber band. Remove the bag after a few days and keep your new plant's compost moist.

You will need...

- Leafy plant
- Scissors
- Jar
- Warm water
- Trowel
- Potting compost or soil
- Gloves
- Small stones
- Flowerpot and saucer
- Ruler
- Pencil or stick
- Clear plastic bag
- Rubber band or string

Not all plants will grow from a cutting, and not all cuttings will grow, so try 2 or 3 cuttings. Good plants to use are coleuses (below) and rosemary.

A baby spider plant grows from the main plant and already has roots. Put one in a shallow tub to grow a cutting more quickly.

The Science:
HOW PLANTS GROW

Your cutting is another example of vegetative reproduction (see page 37). It grows roots to absorb water from the soil. Some water travels to the leaves, where it combines with carbon dioxide gas from the air to make food for the plant using sunlight. This process is called **photosynthesis**. As your cutting grows, it sprouts more leaves to make more food.

Plants do most of their growing at their roots, shoots, and leaves, because these areas are vital for their survival.

GLASS GARDEN

Did you know that you can put plants in a sealed jar and they will keep growing? Here's how to make a glass garden...

WARNING!
Soil contains bacteria. Put a bandage on any cuts on your hands, and wear gloves! DON'T pick wild plants in case they're protected by law or are poisonous.

1 Take a large glass jar with a sealable lid. Wash it in soapy water and dry it well.

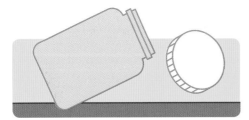

2 Ask an adult to help you collect some soil.

ASK AN ADULT

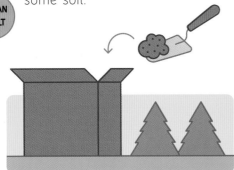

3 Ask an adult to help you dig up some small plants from your yard (or you could buy some from a garden center). Choose a variety of plants to make your garden more interesting (see page 41). Make sure you dig up the roots as well.

ASK AN ADULT

4 Collect a few clumps of moss for your glass garden. Look for it on fallen wood in damp, shady places.

You will need...

- Glass jar (32 to 96 ounces/1 to 3 l)
- Cardboard box
- Trowel
- Gloves
- Soil
- Moss
- Pieces of wood
- Small plants
- Spoon
- Small stones
- Spray bottle
- Water
- Tweezers

PLANT IDEAS

Choose woodland plants that need light, but not direct sunlight. Small, slow-growing plants are best. Flowering plants don't do so well.

- Spider ferns
- Ivy
- Maidenhair fern
- Moss
- Starfish plant
- Nerve plant
- Aquamarine
- Golden clubmoss
- *Helexine* (Baby's Tears)
- "Moon Valley" friendship plant
- Creeping Fig
- *Begonia rex*

5 Find one or two small pieces of fallen wood to make an interesting feature.

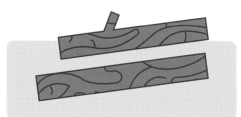

6 Put your jar on its side and spoon in enough small stones to cover the bottom.

7 Sprinkle some soil over the stones. Remember to wear gloves.

8 Spray your plants and wood with water to dampen them.

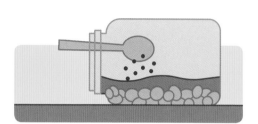

The Science:
HOW PLANTS USE WATER AND GASES

Another name for a glass garden is a terrarium. "Terra" means Earth in Latin, and your glass garden works like a mini planet Earth. The soil and plants in the glass garden lose water molecules by evaporation. The water vapor cools and **condenses** on the glass, and water then trickles down into the soil. On Earth, water vapor condenses into clouds and falls as rain. This is known as the water cycle (see page 73).

In your glass garden, just as in the outside world, the plants take in carbon dioxide gas for photosynthesis, and produce oxygen gas, helping to keep a balance of gases in the air.

Water condenses   Water evaporates

9 Put your wood in the jar, then place your plants on the soil using tweezers. Close the lid and put the jar in a well-lit place, but not in direct sunlight or it will get too hot.

EVERLASTING FLOWERS

Some flowers last only a few days, but by pressing them you can make them last a lifetime. Here's how to do it...

1 Pick a variety of garden flowers—ask an adult first—or buy a bunch of flowers.

ASK AN ADULT

2 Look at the Flower Structures box, then look at your flowers through a magnifying glass. Can you see sepals, petals, stamens, or carpels?

3 Spread a sheet of newspaper on a board and lay your flowers on the newspaper. Put another sheet of newspaper on top of the flowers and weigh it down with a few heavy books.

Make sure the flowers are not touching.

FLOWER STRUCTURES

Flowers come in all shapes and sizes, but they have these structures:

Stamen: a stalk and a blob containing dusty pollen

Ovary: the place where seeds form

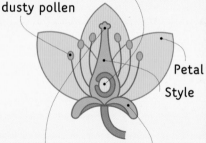

Petal

Style

Stigma: a sticky pad that receives pollen from insects

Sepals: little leaves ringing the base of petals. These are the remains of the flower buds.

Carpel: the structure containing the stigma, style, and ovary

Some flowering plants have many little flowers on a single head.

You will need...

- Fresh flowers
- Magnifying glass
- Old newspapers
- Piece of board
- Heavy books

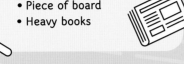

The Science:
HOW FLOWERS WORK

For flowers to produce seeds, the pollen from the stamens of one flower must be transferred to the carpels of another flower. For most garden flowers, insects do this job. An insect is attracted to a flower by its bright color and scent. When it lands on the flower, pollen sticks to it. The insect then visits another flower and the pollen rubs off on the flower's stigma. The insect is rewarded with a sugary drink called nectar found in the base of the flower. The pollen grows into the ovary and helps to form a seed, which can grow into a new plant.

4 Wait at least four weeks before you remove the flowers; it will take that long for them to dry out.

BARK RUBBING

A tree is a giant plant, but why is it covered in tough stuff? A tree's bark is like its fingerprint! Let's investigate by making bark rubbings.

1 Get your tree detective notebook and pen ready! Now, find a tree with textured bark. Note the location of the tree, what type of tree it is (if you know), and the date.

2 Examine the tree's bark with a magnifying glass. Is anything growing on the bark? Are there any bugs on it? Jot down your findings in your notebook.

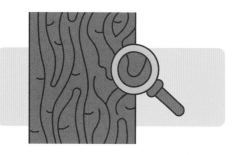

3 Gently scratch the bark with the side of a coin, but try not to damage the bark. Give it a sniff! Does it have a strong scent?

4 Take a sheet of paper and hold it against the tree trunk.

5 Hold the side or blunt end of a crayon against the paper and rub. The pattern of the bark should appear.

6 Repeat steps 4 and 5 for a different tree. Use a different color crayon. Compare your bark rubbings.

It's best to lay the paper lengthways against the trunk and rub the crayon up and down. Take care: if you press too lightly, the pattern may not appear. If you press too hard, the paper may tear.

You will need...

- Notebook
- Pen
- Magnifying glass
- Coin
- Printer size white paper
- Wax crayons

The Science: TREE BARK

Bark is the dead outer layers of a tree trunk. It has two vital jobs: first, it helps to hold up the tree and stop it collapsing under its own weight. Secondly, bark keeps out harmful insects, fungi, and bacteria. (As you may have found out, that doesn't stop some bugs and smaller plants from living on bark.) Some trees shed bark to remove harmful pests. Other trees store chemicals in their bark to kill bacteria and stop the bark from rotting.

As a tree grows, its bark stretches and cracks. Each **species** of tree has a different type of bark.

Tree trunk challenge

This is a challenge for yourself and a friend. Select a number of trees and compare their bark. Ask your friend to close their eyes and turn around three times. With their eyes still closed, lead them to a tree. Can your friend identify the tree by touching its bark? Now swap places with your friend and see how well you do.

SNAIL RACING

Welcome to the world's s-l-o-w-e-s-t sport.
On your marks, get set, and...SQUIRM!

1 Ask an adult to make some holes in the lid of a plastic pot. Put some lettuce leaves in the pot.

ASK AN ADULT

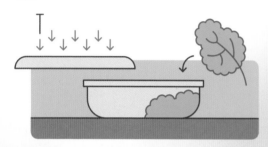

2 Find two snails; they often hide in dark, damp places. Put them in the pot and put the lid on. Place the pot in a dark place for 20 to 30 minutes.

3 Fill a bucket with water and pour it over some paving stones to wet them—but don't flood the place!

4 Place two small stones about 39 inches (1 m) apart on the paving stones.

5 Place a snail next to each stone. Give them 10-15 minutes to get moving. Study them with a magnifying glass. Can you see how they move? Can you see the main parts of their bodies?

This activity works best at dusk on a damp evening.

You will need...

- Nail or other pointed object
- Clean plastic pot with lid
- Lettuce leaves
- Two snails
- Bucket
- Water
- Two small stones
- Tape measure
- Magnifying glass
- Watch

If you don't have a tape measure, you can mark a length of string at 2-inch (5-cm) intervals and use that instead.

6 Measure the distance that each snail travels from its starting stone in 30 minutes. The winner is the snail that travels farthest!

7 After the race, return the snails to the places you found them.

DID YOU KNOW?

In 1995 Archie the snail moved 13 inches (33 cm) in two minutes. It was the world's fastest snail.

The Science:
SNAIL MOVEMENT

Snails belong to a group of animals called mollusks. Most mollusks live in the sea. Garden snails live on land, but they do like damp conditions, which is why you put water on their racetrack.

Unlike us, snails don't have legs. A wave of squeezing muscle movement passes along the foot and the snail moves forward on a trail of slime.

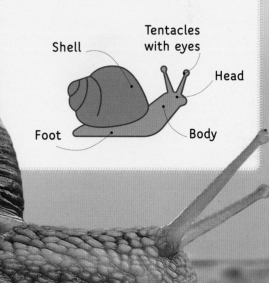

Shell

Tentacles with eyes

Head

Foot

Body

SUPER-STRONG SHELLS

Snails might be small and slow, but their shells are super strong. Let's find out how strong...

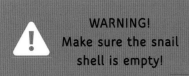

WARNING!
Make sure the snail shell is empty!

1 Weigh a flowerpot and note down its weight. Then weigh some small food cans and check that the weight on the labels is correct.

2 Find an empty snail shell and weigh it. Put it on a firm surface and balance the flowerpot on top of it. You will need to put rocks or books on either side to steady the flowerpot, but make sure they don't support its weight.

3 One by one, add cans to the flowerpot until the shell breaks.

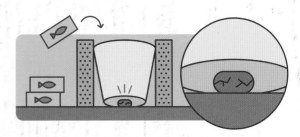

4 Do this sum: weight of cans + weight of flowerpot = weight needed to break the shell!

Chalky shell challenge:

Use the back of a spoon to crush the bits of snail shell to a powder. Cover the powder with 3 $\frac{1}{2}$ ounces (100 ml) of white vinegar. After 15-20 minutes, examine the liquid with a magnifying glass. Can you see bubbles and hear fizzing? The bubbles are carbon dioxide gas made by the chemical reaction between vinegar acid and the chalky shell. It's a similar chemical reaction to the one on page 31.

You will need...

- Kitchen scales
- Empty flowerpot
- Notebook
- Pencil
- Small food cans
- Empty snail shell
- Rocks or books
- Calculator
- White vinegar
- Magnifying glass

The Science:
SNAIL SHELLS

Considering how light they are, snail shells are amazingly strong. They can support hundreds of times their own weight without breaking. The secret is their domed shape, which directs the force of the weight down its sides, preventing the shell from breaking in just one place. Helmets and domed buildings are strong for the same reason.

DID YOU KNOW?

African giant snails can grow to almost 16 inches (40 cm) long. They're the biggest snails on Earth.

WANDERING WOODLICE

Woodlice are not brainy beasts, but they do know what they want and they're happy to show you. Let's find out what woodlice want...

1 Wrap black insulating tape around the bottom half of a tall jar.

2 Attach a black lid to the base of the jar with tape.

3 Catch a woodlouse! You'll find one in a damp corner, usually under a stone. Examine it with a magnifying glass. Can you see its main body parts?

4 Gently place the woodlouse in the bottom of the jar and put the lid on.

5 Put a 1-inch (2.5-cm) wide ball of adhesive putty on a firm surface. Rest the bottom of the jar on the putty, as shown.

Parts of a woodlouse

Close-up of a woodlouse:

Head

Armor

Antennae (feelers)

14 legs

You will need...

- Black insulating tape
- Jar (at least 8 inches/20 cm tall) with lid
- Black lid (to cover jar base)
- Tape
- Woodlouse or pill bug
- Magnifying glass
- Scissors
- Adhesive putty

If you don't have any insulating tape or a black lid, you could use black paper and secure it with tape.

The Science: ARTHROPODS AND PHOTOTAXIS

Woodlice are not insects, but like insects they belong to a larger group of animals called arthropods; arthropod means "jointed foot". Did you spot your woodlouse's jointed legs at step 3? Spiders and crabs are also arthropods.

Woodlice eat rotting wood and plant matter, which helps to recycle food molecules from dead wood into the soil. Not many creatures eat woodlice becasue they taste awful and have protective armor. But they also dry out, so they head for dark places, which are often damp. When a creature moves to or from light, it's called phototaxis.

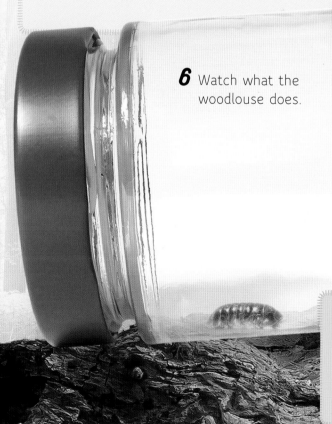

6 Watch what the woodlouse does.

7 When you've finished the experiment, be sure to return your woodlouse to the place you found it.

DID YOU KNOW?

Like other animals, woodlice can't actually digest rotting wood. They need bacteria in their guts to do this job.

GIANT SPIDER'S WEB

Are you brave enough to discover scary spider secrets? Find out as you weave your very own giant web!

1 Find a spot where you can attach your web at eight points (see circle opposite). Each anchor point should be at least 39 inches (1 m) from the next one.

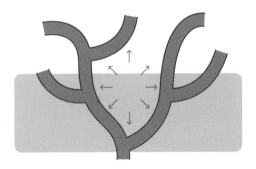

2 Cut a length of string about 47 inches (1.2 m) long.

3 Tie or pin one end of the string to an anchor point. Pull it across to the opposite point and attach it in place. Mark the center point of the string.

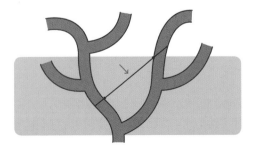

4 Repeat steps 2 and 3, but twist the new string around the center point before you attach the loose end to its anchor point. Repeat with two more strings, keeping them taut. These are called radial threads.

5 Repeat step 2. This time tie the string about halfway along a radial thread and take it around toward the central point in a spiral. Each time you cross a radial string, wrap the string you are holding around it. Try to keep the strings tight.

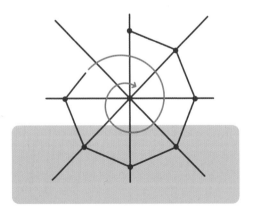

6 Trim any untidy ends with scissors. As a finishing touch, tie a toy spider to the web!

You will need...

- Ball of string
- Scissors
- Tape measure
- Push pins
- Pen
- Toy or paper spider

The Science:
SPIDER WEBS

Congratulations! You've spun a web just like a real spider. Spiders start with the radial threads and then add spiral threads. The spiral threads are sticky and keep the radial threads taut. Although spider silk is very light, it is strong enough to hold insects caught on the sticky threads. Spiders also use silk for wrapping up victims and making nests.

You could attach your web to a doorway or fence using push pins. Or try tying the strings to a garden arch or tree branches. If a string breaks, just tie the ends together and keep going.

DID YOU KNOW?

Some spiders use silk threads to fly far through the air, blown by the wind.

BIRD BREAKFAST

Make a bird feeder to help make life easier for wild birds. Then turn the page to find a delicious bird breakfast recipe...

The best time to do this project is in the winter, when birds are hungry. Don't try it in the spring when birds are feeding their chicks. The growing chicks need insects and worms rather than the food you put out.

1 Take a box and draw a cutting line around it 1 ½ inches (4 cm) from the bottom. Cut off and discard the top of the box.

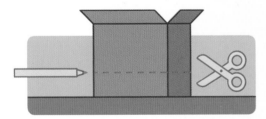

2 Ask an adult to make a hole in each side of the box using a push pin and the ends of a pair of scissors.

ASK AN ADULT

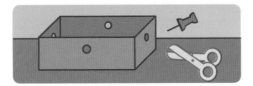

3 Cut two 24-inch (60-cm) lengths of string. Thread one of them through one of the holes from the outside; it may help to push it through the hole with the point of a pencil. Knot the end around the string, as shown.

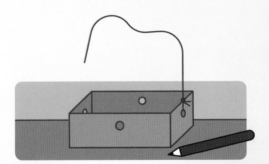

4 Thread the other end of the string through the opposite hole from the outside, and tie it to the string.

5 Take the other length of string, thread it through the two unused holes, and tie the ends as before. Add some bird seed to the feeder.

You will need...

- Box or carton (34 ounces/1 liter)
- Pen
- Ruler
- Scissors
- Push pin
- String
- Pencil
- Bird seed

The best place to hang the bird feeder is from a thin branch that cats can't get to. Choose a branch that you can see from a window so you can watch the birds from indoors using binoculars.

6 Ask an adult to hang the feeder from a thin branch.

ASK AN ADULT

The Science: BIRD FEEDING

Birds need high-energy food because they use so much energy flying and keeping warm. Normally they'll seek out seeds or insects and worms, but these foods are scarce in winter and they'll be happy to eat your food. Seeds are a high-energy food and are ideal for many adult birds.

Hang this bird food next to your bird feeder to attract even more visiting birds!

You will need...

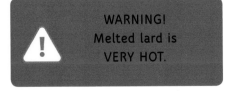

- Plastic cup
- Scissors
- String
- Tape measure
- Bread
- Grater
- Bowl
- Heatproof bowl
- Tablespoon

- Lard, suet, or goose fat
- Microwave oven
- Oats
- Finely chopped nuts
- Pumpkin or sunflower seeds
- Dessert spoon
- Teaspoon

1 Ask an adult to make a hole in the bottom of a plastic cup using scissors, as shown.

ASK AN ADULT

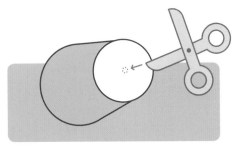

WARNING!
Melted lard is
VERY HOT.

2 Cut a 24-inch (60-cm) length of string. Thread one end through the hole and tie the other end to a short stick. Leave the stick dangling outside the cup.

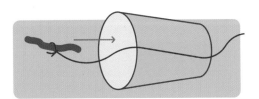

4 Add 2 tablespoons of lard to a heatproof bowl. Ask an adult to microwave the lard for about 30 seconds.

ASK AN ADULT

5 Ask an adult to remove the bowl of lard from the microwave. Stir in the breadcrumbs and one tablespoon of oats. Stir in a dessert spoon each of nuts and seeds. The mixture should be dry and greasy. If it is too runny, stir in some more oats.

ASK AN ADULT

3 Grate half a slice of stale bread into a bowl. Use scissors to snip any large lumps into smaller pieces.

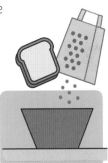

6 Scoop the mixture into the cup and press it down. Pull the string so the stick sits on top of the mixture.

Birdwatch challenge:

Using a pair of binoculars and a bird identification book, can you identify which species of birds are visiting? Which birds prefer which food? Sometimes birds squabble over food. Which birds win these contests?

7 Leave the cup in the fridge for three hours or until the mixture is hard. Turn the cup upside-down and press the base of the cup. If the mixture doesn't slide out, ask an adult to cut open the cup.

ASK AN ADULT

8 Tie the bird cake's string to a branch near your bird feeder.

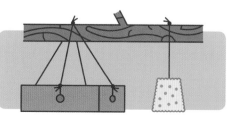

MAKE A WINDSOCK

You can feel it but you never see it. It's always around, but it never stays still. Where does wind come from? Here's one way to find out!

1 Ask an adult to cut a 1-inch (2.5-cm) wide ring from the center of a 2 liter plastic bottle. The edges of the ring should be as smooth and straight as possible.

ASK AN ADULT

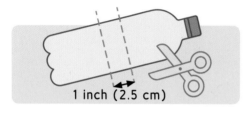

1 inch (2.5 cm)

2 Ask an adult to press and flatten the ring, and then make two holes on opposite sides; they could do this with scissor points or a hole puncher.

ASK AN ADULT

3 Cut a 16-inch (40-cm) length of string and thread it through the holes. Tie the ends together to make a loop.

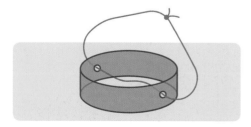

4 Use a ruler and marker to draw 12 to 15 thin strips on a plastic bag, about $^3/_4$ inch (2 cm) wide and 20 inches (50 cm) long. Cut them out.

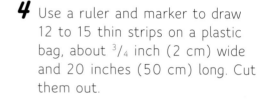

5 Hang the loop up and drape one of the plastic strips over the ring. Tie the strip so the knot is on the ring's bottom edge.

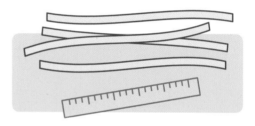

6 Repeat step 5 with the rest of the strips. Try to space them evenly around the ring.

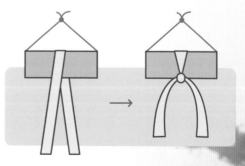

You will need...

- 2 liter plastic bottle
- Small scissors
- Hole puncher
- String
- Plastic bag, such as a garbage bag
- Marker
- Ruler
- Compass

The Science:
WIND AND AIR PRESSURE

Wind is caused by differences in air pressure. Air only moves from areas with high air pressure to places with lower air pressure. In areas of high pressure, cooler air spirals toward the ground. In areas of low pressure, warmer air near the ground spirals upward.

7 Hang your windsock where it will catch the wind. The strips will blow out like streamers, showing which direction the wind is blowing. The stronger the wind, the more it will blow sideways.

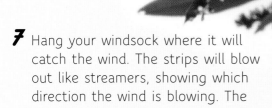

Wind diary challenge:

Keep a wind diary for a week. Check your windsock every morning and evening and note whether the wind is zero, light, medium, or strong. Use a compass to find out which direction the wind is blowing from.

MEASURE THE SUN

The Sun is 93 million miles (150 million km) away. But did you know you can measure the Sun's diameter from outdoors?

1 Use a ruler and pencil to draw two parallel lines across a sheet of paper. The lines should be exactly $1/10$ inch (2.5 mm) apart.

Make sure the pencil is sharp

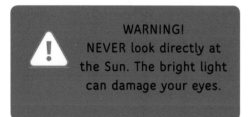

2 Cut a 4 x 6 inches (10 x 15 cm) piece of cardstock. Cut a 1 inch (2.5 cm) square in the cardstock and tape a piece of aluminum foil over the square. Use a push pin to make a hole in the foil.

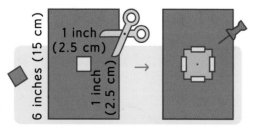

6 inches (15 cm)

1 inch (2.5 cm)

1 inch (2.5 cm)

4 inches (10 cm)

3 Turn the cardstock over and fold down a 1 inch (2.5 cm) flap. Tape the cardstock to the ruler so it lines up with the 10 ¾ inch (27.5 cm) mark.

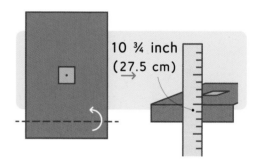

10 ¾ inch (27.5 cm)

4 On a sunny day, put the paper on a table outdoors. The paper should be level with the zero mark on the ruler. Position the card so that its shadow falls on the paper. Move the paper until you see a small, bright circle between the parallel lines. This is an image of the Sun made by sunlight shining through the pinhole.

5 Do these sums to figure out the diameter of the Sun:

For miles: 10.75 ÷ 0.1 = A
93,000,000 ÷ A = ?

For km: 27.5 ÷ 0.25 = A
149,600,000 ÷ A = ?

You will need...

- Ruler
- Paper
- Sharp pencil
- Cardstock
- Scissors
- Aluminum foil
- Tape
- Pin
- Calculator
- Pencil

The Science:
THE DIAMETER OF THE SUN

The aim of the experiment was to measure the diameter of the Sun. You did it by projecting an image of the Sun through the hole and onto the paper. The image was $\frac{1}{10}$ inch (2.5 mm) across at a distance of 10.75 inches (27.5 cm). Figure A in your sum was the number of times that $\frac{1}{10}$ inch (2.5 mm) could fit into the distance. Next you divided the real distance to the Sun by figure A to give the diameter of the Sun. Scientists have measured the diameter of the Sun as 864,800 miles (1,391,000 km). Your equipment isn't accurate enough to produce this exact figure, but hopefully you got close!

SHADOW SECRETS

Try this experiment and the one on the next page to find some surprising science secrets lurking in the shadows.

1 Cut a circle of thick cardstock 1 inch (2.5 cm) across. Stick it to the end of a pencil with adhesive putty.

Just for fun, you could decorate the circle to look like a UFO!

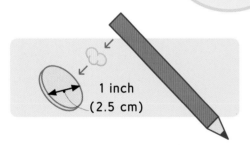

1 inch (2.5 cm)

2 At midday on a sunny day, put a sheet of paper on a flat surface. Hold the pencil 6 inches (15 cm) above the paper—check the distance with a ruler. Make sure the cardstock circle is facing up. Use a colored pen to draw around the circle's shadow.

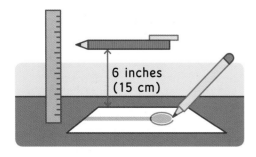

6 inches (15 cm)

3 Repeat step 2 but hold the cardstock circle 12 inches (30 cm) above the paper. Use a different colored pen to draw around the shadow. Measure and compare the two shadow outlines.

4 Darken a room and switch on the light. Once again, measure the shadows made by the circle at 6 inches (15 cm) and 12 inches (30 cm).

5 Can you explain why the shadows in steps 2 and 3 look different than the shadows in step 4?

You could decorate your paper with a little person running away from the scary UFO's shadow!

DID YOU KNOW?

When the Moon passes between the Sun and the Earth, the Moon's shadow passes over Earth and it gets dark. This is called a solar eclipse.

The Science: LIGHT AND SHADOWS

It doesn't matter how far you hold the circle from the paper in sunlight, the shadow always looks the same size. This is because the Sun is very distant, and at midday sunlight hits at right angles. Moving the circle 6 inches (15 cm) nearer the Sun won't block more light, so the shadow stays the same size.

Indoors, things are different. As you raise the circle, its shadow gets bigger and less sharp. It grows because the circle blocks more light as it nears the bulb. At the same time, more light hits the shadow from other angles, making the shadow lighter and more blurred.

This shadow shape-changing experiment works best on a sunny morning or afternoon.

You will need...

- Adhesive putty
- Your circle shape from page 64
- 3 sheets of white printer paper
- Three pens, different colors
- Protractor

1 Place a 1-inch (2.5-cm) wide ball of adhesive putty on a surface. Stick the pencil and cardstock circle from pages 64-65 into the adhesive putty.

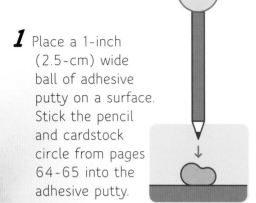

2 Position the pencil so that the circle's shadow falls on the paper. Draw around the shadow in colored pen.

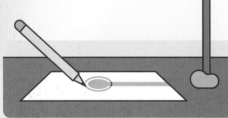

3 Use a protractor to lean the pencil at a 60 degree angle from the surface. Draw around the shadow in a different colored pen.

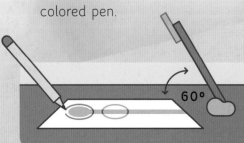

4 Put another sheet of white printer paper on the surface with its edge touching the adhesive putty. Bend and flex the paper to make the pencil's shadow wider. Can you make the pencil's shadow bend?

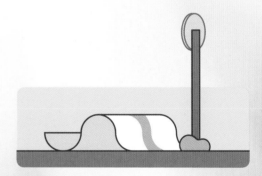

5 Fold the paper on alternate sides to make it corrugated. Each fold should be 1 inch (2.5 cm) apart.

6 Hold the paper up so it forms a staircase with a shadow falling on it. What shape is the shadow?

You should try this experiment around midday.

The Science:
SHADOWS AND ANGLES

Your experiment shows how the length and shape of shadows change with the angle between the light and the surface. A shadow lengthens when the Sun sinks, and it also lengthens if the Sun strikes at an angle.

SHADOW TIME

Who needs clocks? All you need is a sunny day and a helpful shadow to tell you the time! Find out how to make a sun clock, or sundial.

1 Use a ruler to draw a right-angled triangle on a piece of cardstock, as shown.

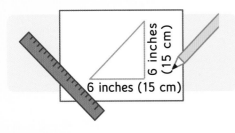

6 inches (15 cm)
6 inches (15 cm)

2 Add a $^5/_8$-inch (1.5-cm) wide rectangle, as shown.

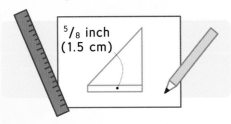

$^5/_8$ inch (1.5 cm)

3 Cut out the shape, then cut a concave curve in the side of the triangle. Fold the rectangle over to make a tab.

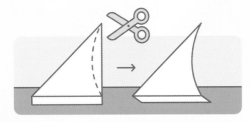

4 Tape the tab to a board so the triangle stands up straight. Use a compass to find north. Point the vertical side of the card triangle toward north. (If you live in the southern hemisphere, point the vertical side to the south.)

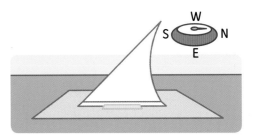

W
S   N
E

DID YOU KNOW?

One of the world's largest sundials is in Jaipur, India. It's nearly 89 feet (27 m) high!

You will need...

- Ruler
- Printer-size sheet of cardstock
- Pencil
- Scissors
- Tape
- Board at least 16 inches (40 cm) square
- Compass

5 Every hour, put a mark where the tip of the triangle's shadow falls on the board. Write the time next to the mark. At the end of the day, you can join up the marks with a curved line.

The Science:
THE EARTH AND THE SUN

We get night and day as the Earth spins in space. Our planet takes 24 hours to turn around. When the part of the Earth you are on is facing the Sun, it's day. And when your part of the Earth is facing away from the Sun, it's night.

As the Earth turns, the angle between the Sun and your triangle shape changes, and its shadow moves in a curve. Since the position of the shadow on each hour doesn't change much from day to day, you've created a sun clock, or sundial.

Tomorrow you can use it to tell the time, if it's still sunny!

● 2:00 pm

Set up this experiment early on a sunny morning. If your sundial leans to one side, you could prop it on each side with a couple of stones.

MAKE A RAINBOW

Why wait for rain? Here are two easy ways to make rainbows!

1 Ask an adult to wash out a spray bottle. Fill it with water.

ASK AN ADULT

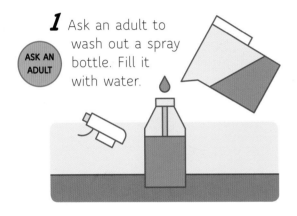

2 Stand with your back to the Sun facing a dark surface. Spray water fast and look for rainbows!

3 Put a sheet of white paper on a clipboard. Use adhesive putty to attach a clear plastic pen tube to the paper.

4 Stand with your back to the Sun. Lean the top of the clipboard toward you and use a magnifying glass to look for rainbow patterns in the shadow under the pen tube.

WARNING!
NEVER use a spray bottle that has held chemicals. Ask an adult to wash the bottle. DON'T spray toward eyes. Avoid breathing the spray.

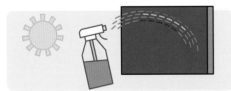

If you can't see any rainbows at step 4, try a different make of pen tube.

You will need...

- Clean plastic spray bottle
- Water
- White paper
- Clipboard
- Adhesive putty
- Clear plastic pen tube
- Magnifying glass

The Science: LIGHT AND REFRACTION

Light is a type of electromagnetic radiation. It transfers energy from a source such as the Sun as it travels in waves. The color of the light depends on the **wavelength** of the wave. Sunlight is white; it's a mix of all the colors of light.

As sunlight enters a raindrop, it slows and bends. Because different wavelengths bend at slightly different angles, the colors in sunlight separate and you see a rainbow. Bending light in this way is called refraction. In steps 3 and 4, the sunlight refracts as it passes from air to the plastic.

You can make amazing rainbows by spraying water from a hose (ask permission first). If the hose doesn't have a spray nozzle, just put your thumb over the end.

RAINY DAY SCIENCE

You don't need sun for outdoor science. Rainy days are just as good! Here's how to make a rain gauge.

1 Prepare your seven-day rain diary as shown.

DATE	WATER LEVEL (in.)	INCREASE (in.)

2 Ask an adult to cut the top third off a 2 liter plastic bottle. It helps to make a small hole before cutting with large scissors. Ask them to trim the cut edge with small scissors.

ASK AN ADULT

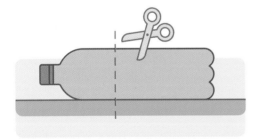

3 If the base of the bottle is uneven, press some modeling clay into the bottom of the bottle to make a flat surface.

4 Remove the cap and turn the top half of the bottle upside down. Place it inside the lower half of the bottle.

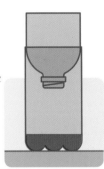

5 Tape the ruler to the lower half of the bottle, making sure it is straight. The zero mark should be level with the top of the modeling clay.

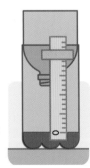

6 Place your rain gauge where rain will fall into it. Wedge bricks or flowerpots around it to stop it from blowing over.

7 Every evening, check the water level in the gauge and write the figure in your diary. If the level has risen, write the difference between the present level and yesterday's level in inches.

You will need...

- Notebook
- Pencil
- 2-liter clear plastic bottle
- Large scissors
- Small scissors
- Modeling clay or jelly
- Wide tape, ideally clear outdoor tape
- See-through ruler

At step 3, you can use jelly instead of modeling clay to make a really flat surface. Let it set overnight in the bottle.

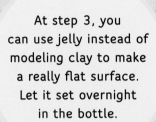

The Science:
RAIN AND THE WATER CYCLE

We saw a water cycle in the glass garden (page 43): here's how it works. Water molecules evaporate into the air from rivers, lakes, and seas. As air is warmed by the Sun, it rises, only to cool again as it gets higher.

As the air cools, the water molecules condense to form clouds of droplets. If the droplets are heavy enough, they fall as rain. The rain flows back into the rivers, lakes, and seas.

DID YOU KNOW?

In 1966, nearly 71 inches (1.8 m) of rain fell in just 24 hours on the island of Réunion.

MOON MISSION

The Moon is in space, but how far away is it from Earth? Here's how you can see the distance between them in relation to their size!

You'll need an area of paving or path 14 feet (4.3 metres) long. Alternatively you can stick the Earth and Moon to a long wall or fence.

1 Using a compass, draw a 1½-inch (3.8 cm) wide circle on a sheet of paper. This is your Moon. Cut it out and color it gray. You could draw on craters too.

2 On another sheet of paper, draw a 5½-inch (14 cm) wide circle. This is your Earth. Cut it out and color it blue. You could add continents and clouds, too.

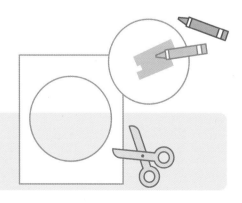

3 Make a stand for your Earth and Moon from cardboard. Make one slightly larger than the other.

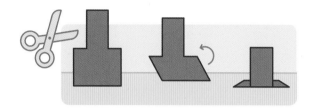

4 Tape the smaller stand to the Moon and the larger one to the Earth.

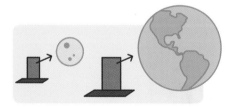

5 Place the Moon at one end of the paved area.

6 Do these sums:
5.5 x 30 = ?
Divide your answer by 12.
The answer is the distance to measure in feet in step 7.

You will need...

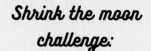

- Compass
- Pencil
- Two sheets of white printer paper
- Crayons, paints, or colored pens
- Ruler
- Scissors
- Cardboard
- Tape
- Calculator
- Tape measure
- Chalk

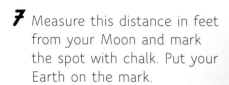

Shrink the moon challenge:

When the full Moon is near the horizon, roll a tube of paper. Put the tube to one eye and close the other. The Moon seems to shrink!

For unknown reasons, the Moon appears 50 percent larger when you can see other nearer objects. By looking through the tube, you shut out other objects and see the Moon at its real size.

7 Measure this distance in feet from your Moon and mark the spot with chalk. Put your Earth on the mark.

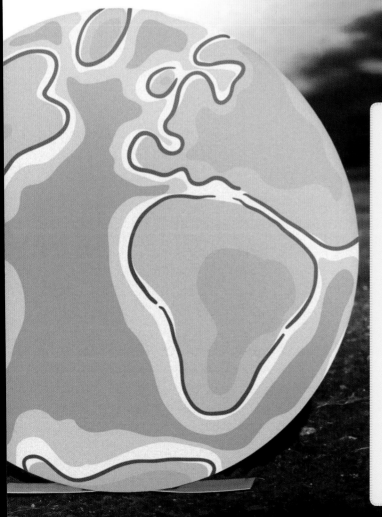

The Science:
THE MOON AND THE EARTH

You've made an accurate plan of the Moon and Earth. The diameter of Earth is about 3.67 times that of the Moon, and the average distance from the Earth to the Moon is about 238,900 miles (384,400 km) —that's 30 times the diameter of Earth. You may be surprised just how small the Moon is compared to Earth and how distant it is. On your plan, the Moon should be 13 feet 9 inches (4.20 m) from your Earth!

MAP THE STARS

Astronomers spend years mapping the stars. You can do it in minutes, and you don't even need a telescope!

FIND A CONSTELLATION

Wait for a clear, moonless night. If you live in the northern hemisphere, see if you can spot the Big Dipper. If you live in the southern hemisphere, look for the Southern Cross.

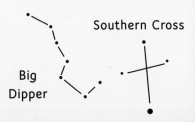

Southern Cross

Big Dipper

2 Wrap a red cloth over the end of a flashlight.

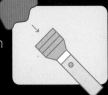

3 Find the **constellation** you're looking for.

4 Ask an adult to hold the flashlight so you can see the cellophane just in front of your face. Look through it at the constellation. Mark the position of each star on the cellophane.

ASK AN ADULT

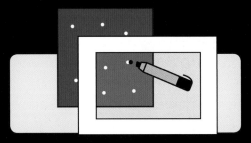

1 To make a frame for your viewer, cut out a rectangle of cardboard. Cut a hole in it and tape some cellophane across the hole. You could decorate the frame.

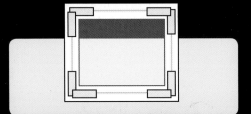

5 Indoors, turn the cellophane over and make felt tip blobs on each of the black blobs you made. Quickly press the felt-tip side on some paper. Lift the cellophane. You've printed a constellation star map! Draw stars over the marks.

You will need...

- Cardboard
- Scissors
- Sheet of cellophane
- Tape
- Small flashlight
- Red cloth
- Black marker
- Water-based felt pens
- White paper

The Science: STARS AND CONSTELLATIONS

Every star, including our Sun, is a giant gas ball. Like our Sun, a star's gravity crushes gas atoms until they fuse together, releasing energy as heat, light, and other types of radiation. Although the stars in a constellation look as if they are all the same distance from us, some are much farther away than others. They're distant from each other in all directions.

If you make a mistake, ask an adult to wipe the marker off the cellophane using white spirit and a kitchen towel.

The final word: OUTDOOR SCIENCE

Science is connected. Everything alive is kept alive by chemical reactions. Animals depend on plants, and plants depend on weather. Animals, the Sun, the Moon, and stars follow the same laws of movement as a flying disk. When you step into the giant science lab of the outdoor world, you're connected too, by knowledge and understanding.

So why not try your own experiments? The FUN is free, the world is waiting. Enjoy!

GLOSSARY

Airfoil A shape with a curved surface when seen in cross-section. Airfoils ensure that wings and helicopter rotors produce lift.

Air pressure The atmosphere above us is pulled toward Earth by gravity. Air pressure is a force acting on an area caused by the weight of the air above us.

Angular momentum The ability of a spinning object to keep spinning. Objects with lots of mass that are spinning quickly have a large angular momentum. Spinning makes an object such as a gyroscope more stable.

Buoyant Able to float or rise upward in water. For this to happen, the upthrust of water must be greater or equal to the force of gravity pulling it down.

Centrifugal effect When an object is turned fast around an axis, it tries to move in a straight line at right angles to the axis. It's called an "effect" because it's not a real force.

Centripetal force The force that pushes a turning object toward the axis of rotation. Without centripetal force, an object would move away in a straight line instead of turning.

Chemical reaction When two or more chemicals combine to make a new molecule or molecules. Some chemical reactions can be reversed; others can't.

Condense When a gas or vapor cools to form liquid droplets. Condensation is the opposite of evaporation.

Constellation A pattern of stars.

Drag Form of friction produced when an object moves through gas or liquid.

Evaporate When a liquid warms and its molecules escape in the form of gas.

Friction A rubbing force produced between moving surfaces or a moving surface in contact with gas or liquid. Friction slows moving objects.

Lift Upward force produced when an object moves through a gas or liquid. Lift can overcome gravity. It helps flying objects gain height.

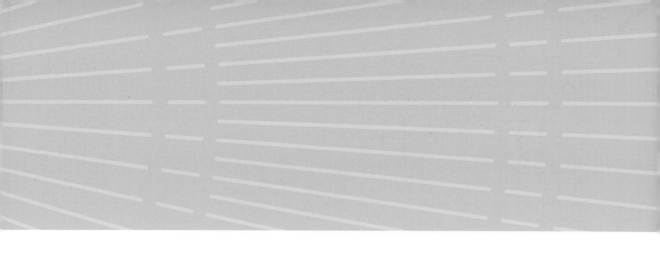

Mass All the matter in an object. Any object that contains atoms has mass.

Molecule A group of atoms bonded together. Most chemicals are made of molecules.

Momentum The ability of a moving object to keep moving. Objects with lots of mass and speed have more momentum than lighter, slower objects.

Photosynthesis How plants turn water and carbon dioxide gas into food using energy from sunlight. Oxygen gas is given off as a by-product.

Sound wave A vibration spreading outward as molecules bump into one another. Sound waves pass through gases, liquids, and solid objects. We experience these vibrations as sounds.

Species A type of animal or plant that can breed successfully with its own kind.

Surface tension A force of attraction between molecules in liquids such as water that makes the liquid form droplets. It also causes water in contact with air to behave like a stretchy skin.

Wavelength Imagine a wavy line; wavelength is the gap between each peak.

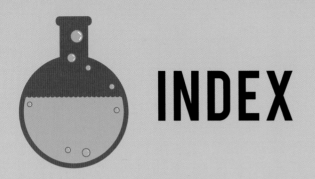

INDEX